Chartreuse

Chartreuse

The Holy Grail of Mixology, with Cocktail Recipes and Lore

MICHAEL TURBACK

FARM
FRESH
BOOKS

DRINKS

INTRODUCTION

"People may say what they like about the decay of Christianity — the religious system that produced green Chartreuse can never really die."

— Hector Hugh Munro

Long, long ago, in the foothills of the Chartreuse Mountains of France, eighty kilometres west of the Italian border, a small group of monks set out to lead lives of contemplation and solitude. Far removed from contact with the outside world, they built a monastery and established the Order of the Carthusians, one of the strictest of the monastic orders, dedicated to prayer and meditation.

Centuries later, a mysterious alchemist arrived at the sequestered monastery and presented the monks with a cryptic formula for a brew of herbs, spices and flowers, promised as "an elixir for long life." The monks mastered production of the medicinal potion, selling bottles in nearby villages to support the Order, and over the years, the fame of the venerable liqueur from Chartreuse spread far and wide.

Throughout history, the Carthusians survived persecutions, revolutions, avalanches, and attempts by the French government to appropriate the sacred recipe. And so the spirit endures, crafted by the willing hands of the monks, whose tradition of silence prevents them from speaking of its secret ingredients.

The more noble Chartreuse is deep emerald green and strong, its intensity tamed by fragrant botanicals and warm spices; her less potent yellow sister is sweeter, with honeyed notes and fruity tones. Complex herbal profiles and vibrant colors of both versions were recognized by the earliest drinksmiths as eminently mixable, versatile, and indispensable in cocktails – delivering exquisite performances when employed in judicious doses.

Chartreuse has its devotees, its white knights, its evangelists. Sir Henry Stanley carried it into the African bush on his way to rescue Dr. Livingstone. French general Charles de Gaulle spiked his bedtime hot chocolate with Chartreuse, and it was a morning pick-me-up for gonzo journalist Hunter S. Thompson. Eccentric actor Bill Murray is known for crashing parties and buying everyone shots of Chartreuse. Slow Food activist Alice Waters cooks with it.

Literature and films are littered with references to it. In F. Scott Fitzgerald's classic novel, Jay Gatsby serves Chartreuse at his glittering parties on Long Island. John Steinbeck's characters sipped martinis made with Chartreuse instead of vermouth in *Sweet Thursday*. And in *Brideshead Revisited*, Evelyn Waugh's hymn to Anglo-Catholicism, his character observes, "There are five distinct tastes as it trickles over the tongue – it's like swallowing a spectrum."

Chartreuse is mentioned in films from Alfred Hitchcock's 1951 *Strangers on a Train* to Quentin Tarantino's 2007 *Death Proof*. Tom Waits croons, "With a pint of Green Chartreuse ain't nothin' seems right, you buy the Sunday paper on a Saturday night," and ZZ Top belts out, "Chartreuse, you got the color that turns me loose." Not to mention Loudon Wainwright III's "Clockwork Chartreuse." Its remarkable tradition, distinctive savor, and divine pedigree have led each in his or her own way to pay homage.

The following pages offer an eclectic collection of 88 drink recipes built on a foundation of the herbal elixir, from pre- and post-Prohibition classics to inventive contemporary notions developed in progressive cocktail programs. For you, dear reader, offered is a book's worth of inspiration and guidance. With this volume as trusted accomplice, you're invited to share in the sensory pleasures of the deeply revered liqueur. Prepare your mind – and your palate – for enlightenment.

A votre santé!

CHARTREUSE COCKTAILS

THE LAST WORD

It's been called "a thinking person's drink," a refreshingly complex sipper that first appeared in Ted Saucier's 1951 *Bottoms Up!* Saucier credits its inception to Frank Fogarty of the Detroit Athletic Club who called it the Last Word because it was usually the final drink of the evening. The cocktail slipped into obscurity until bartender Murray Stenson added it to his menu at Seattle's Zig Zag Café, reintroducing the pale green concoction to the craft of mixology and inspiring stellar variations.

> 3/4 ounce gin
> 3/4 ounce Green Chartreuse
> 3/4 ounce Maraschino liqueur
> 3/4 ounce freshly-squeezed lime juice
> lime peel

Combine liquid ingredients in a mixing glass with cracked ice. Shake vigorously and strain into a coupe glass. Express lime peel over the glass, rub it around the rim, and drop it in.

THE FINAL WARD

Although The Last Word is a drink most would consider impervious to the thought of improvement, New York bartender Phil Ward deviates from the standard formula, replacing gin with rye and lime juice with lemon juice. A deliciously bright and well-balanced alternative, the Final Ward is at once fresh, complex and herbal with the classic interplay of Maraschino and Chartreuse, further deepened by the spicy, aromatic notes of the rye.

> 3/4 ounce rye whiskey
> 3/4 ounce Green Chartreuse
> 3/4 ounce freshly-squeezed lemon juice
> 3/4 ounce Maraschino liqueur
> Maraschino cherry

Combine liquid ingredients in a mixing glass filled with cracked ice. Shake vigorously and strain into a coupe glass. Garnish with cherry.

THE BIJOU

Legendary barman Harry Johnson likely named this drink for colors of three jewels (*bijous* in French): gin for the diamond, vermouth the ruby, and Chartreuse the emerald – three components that come together agreeably for a refreshing and balanced cocktail. The original recipe called for equal parts gin, vermouth, and Chartreuse, but contemporary adaptations tame both vermouth and Chartreuse. (In Paris, the Ritz Bar version bid *au revoir* to Chartruese, partnering gin with orange curacao and dry vermouth).

> 2 ounces gin
> 1 ounce Green Chartreuse
> 1 ounce Italian vermouth
> 1 dash orange bitters
> lemon peel

Combine liquid ingredients in a mixing glass filled with cracked ice. Shake vigorously and strain into a coupe glass. Express lemon peel over the glass, rub it around the rim, and drop it in.

NUCLEAR DAIQUIRI

Over time, the original Daiquirí created in Cuba in the late 19th century has been tinkered and toyed with, but very rarely has it been improved. However, Australian bartender Gregor De Gruyther brings the Daiquiri into the nuclear age with this potent variation. According to Mr. De Gruyther, the drink is served without garnish because "no garnish can withstand the awesome power of the Nuclear Daiquiri."

> 1 ounce white rum
> 1 ounce freshly-squeezed lime juice
> 3/4 ounce Green Chartreuse
> 1/4 ounce falernum

Combine ingredients in a mixing glass filled with cracked ice. Shake vigorously and strain into a coupe glass.

TIPPERARY COCKTAIL

In the words of a British music hall song popularized during the First World War, "The long, long road to Tipperary is the road that leads me home." A few renditions of a cocktail referencing County Tipperary, Ireland have surfaced in vintage cocktail books. This example from Hugo Ensslin's 1916 *Recipes for Mixed Drinks* is considered the most definitive and eminently sippable.

> 2 ounces Irish whiskey
> 3/4 ounce Italian vermouth
> 1/2 ounce Green Chartreuse
> lemon peel

Combine liquid ingredients in a mixing glass filled with cracked ice. Stir for 10 seconds and strain into a cocktail glass. Express lemon peel over the glass, rub it around the rim, and drop it in.

WAITS AND MEASURES

In *Heartattack and Vine*, Tom Waits tells of craziness fueled by "a pint of Green Chartreuse," where "nothin' seems right." Chartreuse has that sort of reputation, according to Dave Shenaut of Portland's Rum Club. The drinksmith takes inspiration from the classic Bijou (normally served cold) and gives it a toddy twist, resulting in a powerfully-flavored winter warmer.

> 1 1/2 ounces Bacardi rum
> 1 1/2 ounces Bonal Gentiane-Quina
> 1/2 ounce Martinique rum
> 1/2 ounce Yellow Chartreuse
> 1/2 ounce honey syrup*
> 2 ounces boiling water
> orange wheel, studded with 2 cloves

Rinse a toddy mug with boiling water to preheat, then add liquid ingredients and stir to combine. Garnish with orange wheel.

*Combine 1 cup honey and 1 cup water in a small saucepan over medium heat and stir until sugar dissolves. Remove from heat, let cool to room temperature and transfer to a clean glass jar.

JIMMIE ROOSEVELT

In 1939, *Town and Country* magazine sent Charles H. Baker Jr. on assignment around the world to find the very best food and drink. The result was *The Gentleman's Companion*, a grand cocktail tour that takes the reader on imaginative flights fueled by drinks like the Champagne cocktail he christened after the oldest son of President Franklin D. Roosevelt. "It is cooling, refreshing, invigorating, a delight to the eye and palate," writes Baker.

> 1 barspoon powdered sugar
> 5 dashes Angostura bitters
> 2 ounces Cognac
> Champagne, chilled
> 2 tablespoons Green Chartreuse

Fill a big 16-ounce thin crystal goblet with finely cracked ice. Saturate the sugar with bitters and place in the center. Add Cognac and top up with Champagne. Carefully float Chartreuse over the top.

PERPETUAL SUNRISE

The mystical union of gin, Italian vermouth and Campari was conceived and popularized at the Caffé Casoni in Florence's famed Palazzo Strozzi, a hub of Anglo-Florentine sophistication during the interwar years. The traditionally simple, yet powerful recipe from Brooklyn's Nighthawk Cinema starts with a Chartreuse rinse and replaces Campari with a nip of Fernet-Branca. "Life is a great sunrise," wrote Nabokov.

> 1/2 ounce Green Chartreuse
> 1 1/2 ounces gin
> 1 ounce Italian vermouth
> 1/2 ounce Fernet-Branca

Fill a coupe glass with ice and let it sit until the glass is chilled. Once the glass is chilled, toss the ice, pour in Chartreuse, swirl it around to fully coat the interior walls of the glass, then discard. Combine gin, vermouth, and Fernert-Branca in a mixing glass with cracked ice. Stir for 10 seconds and strain into the prepared glass.

HARRY DENTON MARTINI

In San Francisco, they say it's not a party unless Harry Denton is there. A man *The San Francisco Chronicle* calls one of the city's most visible bon vivants, and promoter and owner of several successful establishments, including The Starlight Club atop the St. Francis Hotel, Denton once explained, "The bar is the grandest stage in the world and the bartender brings it to life every night." His martini has become a San Francisco classic.

>   1 1/4 ounces gin
>   1/2 ounce Green Chartreuse

Combine ingredients in a mixing glass filled with cracked ice. Shake vigorously and strain into a martini glass.

NORWEGIAN WOOD

Created by Jeffrey Morgenthaler of Portland's Clyde Common, its name is less about the Beatles song and more about the Japanese novel it inspired. In the title of *Noruwei no Mori* by Haruki Murakami, *Mori* translates as wood of the "forest," and forest settings and imagery are significant in the story. In crafting the cocktail, Morgenthaler combines savory herbs of the Scandinavian spirit and fruit of applejack with the woodsy, herbal, floral notes of Chartreuse jaune. It is said that going into the woods is going home.

> 1 ounce aquavit
> 1 ounce Laird's Applejack
> 3/4 ounce Italian vermouth
> 1/4 ounce Yellow Chartreuse
> 1 dash Angostura bitters
> lemon peel

Combine liquid ingredients in a mixing glass filled with cracked ice. Stir for 10 seconds and strain into a cocktail glass. Express lemon peel over the glass, rub it around the rim, and drop it in.

DIAMONDBACK

Ted Saucier, the publicist for the Waldorf-Astoria hotel in New York, collected the best of Truman-era's cocktails from a variety of sources, celebrities to bar staff. He discovered this drink in the now-defunct Diamondback Lounge, one level down from the lobby of Baltimore's Lord Baltimore Hotel. (The Diamondback Terrapin turtle is the state reptile and official mascot of the University of Maryland).

> 1 1/2 ounces rye whiskey
> 3/4 ounce Laird's Applejack
> 3/4 ounce Yellow Chartreuse
> mint sprig

Combine liquid ingredients in a mixing glass filled with cracked ice. Shake vigorously and strain into a cocktail glass. Garnish with mint sprig.

CE SOIR

Vincent Van Gogh wrote, "I often think that the night is more alive and more richly colored than the day." This artistic late-night sipper from Nicole Lebedevitch of Boston's The Hawthorne tempers intense flavors and bitter edges with herbal, silky, honeyed notes of Chartreuse jaune.

> 2 ounces Cognac
> 3/4 ounce Cynar
> 1/2 ounce Yellow Chartreuse
> 2 dashes orange bitters
> 2 dashes Angostura bitters
> lemon peel

Combine liquid ingredients in a mixing glass filled with cracked ice. Stir for 10 seconds and strain into a snifter glass. Express lemon peel over the glass, rub it around the rim, then discard.

THE PURITAN

By the turn of the last century, European and American palates were becoming accustomed to the refreshing dryness of the new, London-style gins. The Puritan, possibly so named for its dryness, appeared in Frederic Lawrence Knowles' 1900 *The Cocktail Book: A Sideboard Manual for Gentlemen*, a precursor to the Dry Martini.

 1 1/2 ounces gin
 3/4 ounce French vermouth
 1 barspoon Yellow Chartreuse
 3 dashes orange bitters

Combine ingredients in a mixing glass filled with cracked ice. Stir for 10 seconds and strain into a coupe glass.

IRMA LA DOUCE

"This is not just a job, it's a profession," insists the charming
Parisian prostitute in the 1963 comedy *Irma la Douce* starring
Shirley MacLaine. Created by the Ladies United for the Preser-
vation of Endangered Cocktails in Boston, the savory, herbal,
and refreshing drink is named for the racy bright green stock-
ings that Irma wears throughout the film.

> 1/2-inch slice cucumber, peeled
>   + 1 slice for garnish
> 1 1/2 ounces Hendrick's gin
> 1/2 ounce Green Chartreuse
> 1/2 ounce freshly-squeezed lemon juice
> 1/2 ounce grapefruit juice
> 1/4 ounce simple syrup

Muddle cucumber in the bottom of a mixing glass. Fill
with cracked ice and add remaining ingredients. Shake
vigorously and strain into a cocktail glass. Garnish with
cucumber slice.

FEMME FATALE

Chartreuse adds a seasoning of herbs and a brilliant green color that brightens the palate and transforms the classic Martini formula. You can make it dirty by adding a little olive juice if you like, or you can be a little more subtle and add the essence of olives by garnishing with three olives instead.

> 1 1/2 ounces gin
> 1/2 ounce Green Chartreuse
> 1/2 ounce French vermouth
> 1 green olive

Combine liquid ingredients in a mixing glass filled with cracked ice. Stir for 10 seconds and strain into a martini glass. Drop olive into the bottom of the glass.

SIR RIDGEWAY KNIGHT COCKTAIL

"Beer drinkers lead a dreary and gaseous life ... Whiskey enthusiasts are ... confined to a three-lane highway – straight, soda, or just plain water. But the cocktail contriver ... has the whole world of nature at command..." In his 1941 *Cocktail Guide and Ladies' Companion*, Crosby Gaige relates an old mountaineer's tale, in which a mix of brandy and Chartreuse was called the "Club Temperance Drink."

2/3 ounce brandy
2/3 ounce triple sec
2/3 ounce Green Chartreuse
2 dashes Angostura bitters

Combine ingredients in a mixing glass filled with cracked ice. Stir for 10 seconds and strain into a coupe glass.

THE BLENHEIM

Winston Churchill described what he called an absolutely sacred rite: "Smoking cigars and also drinking of alcohol before, after and if need be during all meals and in the intervals between them." The Blenheim cocktail, named for the ancestral home of the British statesman, was created at the the Savoy Hotel's American Bar by Joe Gilmore to mark Sir Winston's ninetieth birthday. (It's also known as the Four Score and Ten).

> 1 1/2 ounces Cognac
> 1 ounce Yellow Chartreuse
> 1/2 ounce Lillet
> 1/2 ounce freshly-squeezed orange juice
> 1/2 ounce Dubonnet

Combine ingredients in a mixing glass filled with cracked ice. Shake vigorously and strain into a cocktail glass.

MIDNIGHT
IN PARIS

"Paris is always a good idea," said Audrey Hepburn. And from Geraldine, Toronto's Parisian-style bistro, Michael Mooney pays homage to the City of Lights with a Chartreuse-instilled, Absinthe-soaked libation, refreshed with cucumber, and animated with sparkling wine from the Jura region of France.

3 slices cucumber + 1 additional for garnish
1 ounce absinthe
1/2 ounce Yellow Chartreuse
3/4 ounce freshly-squeezed lime juice
1/2 ounce simple syrup
Crémant Du Jura Brut (or other dry sparkling
        wine), chilled

Muddle 3 slices of cucumber in the bottom of a mixing glass. Add Absinthe, Chartreuse, lime, simple syrup, and fill with ice. Shake vigorously and double-strain into a Champagne coupe glass. Top up with the sparkling wine and garnish with cucumber slice.

ALASKA COCKTAIL

"So far as can be ascertained," explains Harry Craddock in *The Savoy Cocktail Book* (1930), "this delectable potion is NOT the staple diet of the Esquimaux. It was probably first thought of in South Carolina – hence its name." In 1948's *The Fine Art of Mixing Drinks*, David Embury adds a measure of dry sherry to create an Alaska spinoff called the "Nome." Brrr!

    1 1/2 ounces gin
    1/2 ounce Yellow Chartreuse
    1 dash orange bitters
    lemon peel

Combine liquid ingredients in a mixing glass filled with cracked ice. Stir for 10 seconds and strain into a coupe glass. Express lemon peel over the glass, rub it around the rim, and drop it in.

THE CLOISTER

The cloister is a place of solitude that provides a tranquil environment for the Monks of Chartreuse to meditate and contemplate their path to salvation. A cocktail called The Cloister was first suggested in the 1975 edition of *Playboy's Host & Bar Book* by Thomas Mario. Chartreuse jaune, used sparingly, blends with the citrus and gin into a nicely balanced drink, with a heady bouquet of fresh-cut grapefruit.

> 2 ounces gin
> 1/2 ounce Yellow Chartreuse
> 1/2 ounce freshly-squeezed grapefruit juice
> 1 barspoon freshly-squeezed lemon juice
> 1/2 barspoon powdered sugar

Combine ingredients in a mixing glass filled with cracked ice. Shake vigorously and strain into a cocktail glass.

ILE DE FRANCE SPECIAL

The recipe for this "picker-upper" was passed along to Charles H. Baker by a habitual crosser on the Ile de France ocean liner. In *The Gentlemen's Companion* he recounts, "The bar maitre, one Reynauld, on this somewhat amazing craft has found that picker-uppers have to be even better than putter-downers the night before." And in tasting the drink, Mr. Baker notes, "the pungent herbs greet the nostrils, then the cool quenching of the viney bubbly."

> 1/2 barspoon powdered sugar
> 3/4 ounce Cognac
> Champagne, chilled
> 1 to 2 dashes Yellow Chartreuse

Add sugar and Cognac to a Champagne glass. Fill with Champagne, then top off with Yellow Chartreuse.

CHARTREUSITO

The Mojito is most closely tied to Cuba's famous La Bodeguita del Medio bar visited some years ago by Ernest Hemingway. In its makeup, rum gives the drink a kick, limes contribute thirst-quenching sourness, and mint provides a cooling sensation on the tongue. A measure of Chartreuse adds herbaceous complexity without straying too far from the traditional formula.

> 1 ounce freshly-squeezed lime juice
> 1 tablespoon powdered sugar
> 6 to 8 fresh mint leaves
> 1 ounce light rum
> 1 ounce Green Chartreuse
> club soda, chilled

Muddle the lime juice, sugar, and mint leaves in the bottom of a highball glass. Fill the glass with ice, and add rum and Chartreuse. Top it off with club soda.

SKINNER & EDDY

According to "Luscious" Lucius Beebe (moniker bestowed by Walter Winchell), Crosby Gaige was never known to shy away "when the ice in the shaker called stirringly to duty." His eccentric gin-based cocktail is named in honor of Ned Skinner and John Eddy, World War I shipbuilders, notable for breaking world production speed records for building our big boats.

> 1 ounce gin
> 3/4 ounce Yellow Chartreuse
> 2 dashes orange bitters

Combine ingredients in a mixing glass filled with cracked ice. Stir for 10 seconds and strain into a coupe glass.

PORTO FLIP

"Send this up on the breakfast tray of the tweakiest and most jangled week-end guest on the casualty list and watch the smiles wreathe," writes Charles H. Baker Jr. in *The Gentleman's Companion*. **"Be sure it goes down on an empty tummy for best and most soothing effect."** His version of the classic pick-me-up was credited to the Army and Navy Club in Manila.

> 2 ounces port wine
> 1 whole egg
> 1 ounce heavy cream
> 1 ounce Cognac
> 2 barspoons powdered sugar
> 1 barspoon Green Chartreuse
> grated nutmeg

Combine liquid ingredients in a mixing glass and dry shake. Fill with cracked ice and shake vigorously. Strain into a small goblet. Hold a spoon directly over the drink, rounded side up, and gently pour Chartreuse over the spoon, creating a "float" on top of the drink. Dust with nutmeg.

LUNATICS IN THE GARDEN

"The abandoned monastery still closes around the courtyard, as
though a wound were healing," writes Rainer Maria Rilke.
"Those who live there now also enjoy recess and take no part in
the life outside." Inspired by the verses of the Austria poet,
Alex Conde of Hudson in Oakland, California creates an intense-
ly lyrical twist on The Last Word.

1 ounce egg white
1 ounce gin
1 ounce freshly-squeezed lime juice
3/4 ounce Maraschino liqueur
3/4 ounce Green Chartreuse
1 dash absinthe

Combine ingredients in a mixing glass. Dry shake. Fill
with cracked ice and shake vigorously. Double-strain
into a cocktail glass.

NE PLUS ULTRA

Charles H. Baker Jr., on assignment for *Town and Country* , compiled *The Gentleman's Companion: Being an Exotic Drinking Book or, Around the World with Jigger, Beaker and Flask,* an eclectic collection worthy of Jules Verne's Phileas Fogg, each stop in his travelogue punctuated by a cocktail. Baker called Chartreuse "one of the cordial immortals of all time," and recorded the recipe for a Chartreuse-spiked drink served at La Zaragozana, Havana's oldest restaurant.

> 1/2 ounce Green Chartreuse
> 1/2 ounce apricot brandy
> 1/2 ounce Benedictine
> 1/2 ounce Cointreau
> 1/2 ounce cognac
> 1/2 ounce crème de cacaco
> 1 dash anisette

Combine ingredients in a mixing glass filled with cracked ice. Shake vigorously and strain over new crushed ice in a cocktail glass. Serve with a short straw.

THE LAST WORDS OF OSCAR WILDE

A tribute to Irish poet Oscar Wilde by Justin Taylor of Boulevard Kitchen & Oyster Bar in Vancouver, British Columbia draws inspiration from The Last Word cocktail. The actual last words of Mr. Wilde, as history suggests, are "This wallpaper is terrible, one of us will have to go!" The drinksmith replaces gin with Irish whisky, Maraschino with vanilla oolong syrup, then adds a few dashes of chocolate bitters and some egg whites "to create the wallpaper."

> 1 ounce Irish whisky
> 3/4 ounce Green Chartreuse
> 3/4 ounce oolong syrup*
> 1 ounce freshly-squeezed lime juice
> 2 dashes chocolate bitters
> 3/4 ounce eggwhites
> dried oolong leaves

Combine liquid ingredients in a mixing glass filled with cracked ice. Shake vigorously and double strain into a cocktail glass. Garnish with oolong leaves.

*Bring 2 cups of water to boil in a sauce pan. Add 2 cups of turbinado sugar and 4 tablespoons of tea leaves Reduce to simmer and stir until sugar is dissolved. Remove from heat and let tea steep for 1 hour, or until cool. Remove tea and bottle syrup.

GLOVER'S
MANGE CURE

"In the world of potables, the cocktail represents adventure and experiment," insists Crosby Gaige. "All other forms of drinking are more or less static." His 1941 *Cocktail Guide and Ladies Companion*, described as a serious study of the thoughts of the leading bartenders of his era, includes a mix of two of the more famous medicinal liqueurs invented by monks. "Shake, strain, and rub briskly into the tonsils," suggests Mr. Gaige.

> 1/2 ounce Benedictine
> 1/2 ounce Green Chartreuse
> 1 ounce Laird's Applejack
> 1 dash Angostura bitters

Combine ingredients in a mixing glass filled with cracked ice. Shake vigorously and strain into a coupe glass.

NAKED & FAMOUS

This balanced and refreshing cocktail by Joaquin Simó of Alchemy Consulting is both a deconstruction of the Last Word as well as a twisted homage. It resembles the equal-parts prototype, but tweaks the spirits – smoky mezcal and bitter Aperol kept in check with Chartreuse jaune. The drinksmith describes it as "the bastard child born out of an illicit Oaxacan love affair between the classic Last Word and the Paper Plane."

> 3/4 ounce mezcal
> 3/4 ounce Yellow Chartreuse
> 3/4 ounce Aperol
> 3/4 ounce freshly-squeezed lime juice

Combine ingredients in a mixing glass filled with cracked ice. Shake vigorously and strain into a coupe glass.

BITER COCKTAIL

The name refers to a "biter" or someone who can't formulate good ideas of their own, so they steal from those around them. Since this refreshing, tart and easy-sipping cocktail closely resembles The Last Word, we're not sure who Harry Craddock had in mind when he included the drink in *The Savoy Cocktail Book*.

> 1 1/2 ounces gin
> 3/4 ounce Green Chartreuse
> 3/4 ounce freshly-squeezed lemon juice
> 1/4 ounce simple syrup
> 1 dash absinthe

Combine ingredients in a mixing glass filled with cracked ice. Shake vigorously and strain into a cocktail glass.

CHARTREUSE SWIZZLE

Icy drinks mixed with rum originated in the West Indies, where they were whisked to a froth with a "swizzle-stick" made from the stem of a native plant. Rum Swizzles were the drink of choice at what was purportedly the world's first cocktail party held in London, England in 1924 by novelist Alec Waugh. This modern notion of the primitive Swizzle was created by San Francisco bartender Marcovaldo Dionysos who switches out the traditional rum for Green Chartreuse.

1 1/2 ounces Green Chartreuse
1 ounce pineapple juice
3/4 ounce freshly-squeezed lime juice
1/2 ounce falernum
grated nutmeg
mint sprig

Combine ingredients in a Collins glass filled with crushed ice. Insert a barspoon into the drink and swizzle until frost appears on the outside of the glass. Dust with nutmeg and garnish with mint sprig.

LAPHROAIG PROJECT

In this mixological endeavor, vaguely reminiscent of The Last
Word, Australian bartender Owen Westman achieves balance
and harmony between the smoky peatness of Laphroaig Scotch
and the herbal complexity of Chartreuse. Notes on the finish
are provided by aromatic peach bitters, produced by Fee
Brothers in Rochester, New York.

> 1 ounce Green Chartreuse
> 1 ounce freshly-squeezed lemon juice
> 1/2 ounce Laphroaig Quarter Cask
> 1/2 ounce Maraschino liqueur
> 1/4 ounce Yellow Chartreuse
> 2 dashes peach bitters
> lemon peel

Combine liquid ingredients in a mixing glass filled with
cracked ice. Shake vigorously and strain over new ice
in an Old Fashioned glass. Express lemon peel over the
glass, rub it around the rim, and drop it in.

XANTIPPE

As reported in *The New York Times* in 1913, ladies who frequent New York's Cafe des Beax Arts "insist on having new cocktails made, and they have to be named after something that is interesting – usually a new play, because that is what interests them." That season, a drink took its name from a Broadway show called *Believe Me, Xantippe*. The bartender explained, "You can name a cocktail after the latest fashion in skirts or waists and there will be a heavy run on it."

> 1 ounce vodka
> 1/2 ounce Yellow Chartreuse
> 1/2 ounce cherry brandy

Combine ingredients in a mixing glass filled with cracked ice. Shake vigorously and strain into a cocktail glass.

MARY ROSE

During the War of the Roses, King Henry VIII named an English warship after his favorite sister, Mary Tudor, and the rose as the emblem of the Tudors. While leading an attack on galleys of the French invasion fleet, she sank in the straits north of the Isle of Wight. A drink in her honor was created by Philip Jeffrey at the Great Eastern Hotel Bar in London.

> 1 fresh rosemary sprig
> 2 ounces gin
> 1 ounce Green Chartreuse
> 1/2 ounce simple syrup

Muddle rosemary in the bottom of a mixing glass. Fill with ice and add other ingredients. Shake vigorously and fine-strain into a cocktail glass.

THE BITTER SPARK

In this sparkling cocktail concocted by barman Jonny Almario at San Francisco's Hawthorn Lounge, Chartreuse makes a subtle appearance, just enough to provide drama without turning the drink into a liquid potpourri of herbs. There are always sparks when putting two tyrants – Chartereuse and Fernet-Branca – in the same room.

> 1/2 ounce Green Chartreuse
> 1/2 ounce Fernet-Branca
> 1/2 ounce Amaro Montenegro
> 1/2 ounce Averna
> Prosecco, chilled
> orange peel

Fill a coupe glass with ice and let it sit until the glass is chilled. Once the glass is chilled, toss the ice, pour in Fernet-Branca, swirl it around to fully coat the interior walls of the glass, then discard. Combine Chartreuse, Amaro Montenegro, and Averna in a mixing glass with cracked ice. Stir for 10 seconds and strain into the prepared glass. Top up with Prosecco. Express orange peel over the glass, rub it around the rim, and drop it in.

EVERY-BODY'S IRISH COCKTAIL

An Irish proverb goes like this: "Best while you have it use your breath; there is no drinking after death." In his 1930 *Savoy Cocktail Book*, Harry Craddock explains that his drink was "created to mark, and now in great demand on, St. Patrick's Day." Lenten restrictions on drinking alcohol are lifted for that day, so "drowning the shamrock" has become an integral part of the celebration.

> 1 1/2 ounces Irish whisky
> 1 1/2 ounces French vermouth
> 1/2 ounce Green Chartreuse
> 1/2 ounce green crème de menthe

Combine ingredients in a mixing glass filled with cracked ice. Stir for 10 seconds and strain into a cocktail glass.

PETIT CAFÉ

It's either an elevated take on Irish Coffee or a White Russian turned on its head. H. Joseph Ehrmann of Elixir in San Francisco marries the soothing flavors and textures of coffee liqueur and cream with the sweet, herbal notes of Chartreuse. To borrow the words of Douglas William Jerrold, who compared marriage to a drink, "It should not be properly judged until the second glass."

> 1 1/2 ounces coffee liqueur
> 1 ounce Green Chartreuse
> 1/4 cup heavy cream, lightly whipped
> Demerara sugar

Combine coffee liqueur and Chartreuse in a mixing glass filled with cracked ice. Stir for 10 seconds and strain into a wine glass. Top with whipped cream and garnish with a pinch of Demerara sugar.

WARD'S COCKTAIL

German-born bartender Hugo R. Ensslin self-published *Recipes for Mixed Drinks (1917)*, a compilation whose introduction reads: "The object of this book is to give a complete list of the standard mixed drinks that are in use at present in New York City, with directions for preparing same in the most simple manner to get the best results. It is intended for use in the home, as well as a guide for those employed in hotels, clubs, etc." There's a seductive simplicity in Mr. Ensslin's mix of Chartreuse and Cognac.

> orange slice
> 1 1/2 ounces Green Chartreuse
> 1 1/2 ounces Cognac
> mint sprig

Place orange slice in the bottom of the glass, fill with finely cracked ice. Add the Chartreuse and Cognac. Garnish with mint sprig.

THE FITZGERALD

Nick Carraway enjoys a glass of Chartreuse on the night he first meets the elusive ant-hero in F. Scott Fitzgerald's *The Great Gatsby*: "Finally we came to Gatsby's own apartment, a bedroom and a bath, and an Adam study, where we sat down and drank a glass of some Chartreuse he took from a cupboard in the wall." In this homage to the great American novelist, a martini framed with herbal complexity resonates with the theme of Gatsby's carefully cultivated world.

> 1 1/2 ounces gin
> 1/2 ounce French vermouth
> 1 barspoon Yellow Chartreuse
> 1 dash absinthe
> lemon peel

Combine liquid ingredients in a mixing glass filled with cracked ice. Stir for 10 seconds and strain into a cocktail glass. Express lemon peel over the glass, rub it around the rim, and drop it in.

THE BLUR

"There comes a time in every woman's life when the only thing that helps is a glass of Champagne," Said Bette Davis. In this bubbly brunch cocktail from San Francisco's Nopa – meant to blur the lines between the night before and the morning after – Champagne enlivens the herbaceous Chartreuse, the mixture balanced with an eye-opening pour of tart lime juice and bitter-sweet, almond-flavored liqueur.

> 1 1/2 ounces Green Chartreuse
> 1 1/2 ounces Maraschino liqueur
> 1 1/2 ounces freshly-squeezed lime juice
> Champagne, chilled

Combine Chartreuse, Maraschino, and lime in a mixing glass filled with cracked ice. Shake vigorously and strain into two Champagne flutes, dividing evenly. Top up each flute with Champagne.

DÉMODÉ

"Whiskey, like a beautiful woman, demands appreciation," writes Haruki Murakami. "You gaze first, then it's time to drink." This is no-nonsense counterpart to the traditional Old Fashioned cocktail with bitters-soaked sugar, rye whiskey as the base spirit, and a Chartreuse float – layers of flavors that reward slow, thoughtful sipping.

> 1 sugar cube
> 3 to 4 dashes Angostura bitters
> 2 ounces rye whiskey
> 1 barspoon Green Chartreuse
> lemon peel

In the bottom of an Old Fashioned glass, muddle sugar with Angostura bitters. Add rye and a single big piece of ice. Stir a few times, but don't over dilute. Hold a spoon directly over the drink, rounded side up, and gently pour Chartreuse over the spoon, creating a "float" on top of the drink. Express lemon peel over the glass, rub it around the rim, and drop it in.

PAGO PAGO COCKTAIL

In 1940, the capital of American Samoa was immortalized both in film (*South of Pago Pago* starring Victor McLaglen, Jon Hall and Frances Farmer) and in a cocktail guide called *The How and When*. While fashioned with the exotic-drink essentials of rum, pineapple and lime juice, the Pago Pago magnifies complexity with herbal Chartreuse and notes of chocolate and vanilla from crème de cacao.

> 3 cubes fresh pineapple
> 1/2 ounce freshly-squeezed lime juice
> 1/2 ounce Green Chartreuse
> 1/4 ounce white crème de cacao
> 1 1/2 ounces gold Puerto Rican rum

Combine pineapple, lime juice, Chartreuse and creme de cacao in a cocktail shaker. Muddle thoroughly. Add rum and fill with cracked ice. Shake vigorously and strain into a cocktail glass.

GOLDEN SLIPPER

This simple equation is put forward by Bill Kelly in his 1945 book, *The Roving Bartender*, the "little book for those who don't know and know they don't know." As a founding member of the B. I. L. (Bartenders International League), his motto was "Always remember to treat your brother bartenders with courtesy, and see that they treat you the same.

> 1 ounce Yellow Chartreuse
> 1 ounce brandy
> 1 egg yolk

Combine ingredients in a mixing glass filled with cracked ice. Shake vigorously and strain into a coupe glass.

CHAMPS ÉLYSÉES

Known in France as *La Plus Belle Avenue du Monde* (the most beautiful avenue in the world), the Champs-Élysées is the Parisian center of commerce and culture as well as a source of national pride. A cocktail named for the famous street first appeared in Henry Craddock's 1930 *Savoy Cocktail Book*, although the original recipe doesn't specify Green or Yellow Chartreuse. This ambiguity allows some room to play, so use whichever you prefer.

1 1/2 ounces brandy
1/2 ounce Chartreuse (Green or Yellow)
1/4 ounce freshly-squeezed lemon juice
1/8 ounce simple syrup
2 dashes Angostura bitters

Combine ingredients in a mixing glass filled with cracked ice. Shake vigorously and strain into a coupe glass.

CLUB COCKTAIL

The Gin and It cocktail is short for Gin and Italian, a reference to the Italian sweet vermouth. It's one of the oldest Martini drinks, dating back to the 19th century with many variations, none quite as successful as the simple equation put forward by Bill Kelly in his 1945 book *The Roving Bartender*. Kelly calls for the addition of Yellow Chartreuse, and perhaps just as important is how Kelly serves the drink – as a cocktail to be poured straight up.

> 1 ounce gin
> 1/2 ounce Italian vermouth
> 1/4 ounce Yellow Chartreuse
> 1 dash orange bitters
> lemon peel

Combine liquid ingredients in a mixing glass filled with cracked ice. Stir for 10 seconds and strain into a cocktail glass. Express lemon peel over the glass, rub it around the rim, and drop it in.

TREATY OF PARIS

A cocktail and a history lesson. The autumnal coffee cocktail, created by Michael Cadden of Seattle's Tavern Law, is concocted with a shot of espresso and herbal, darker spirits that give a sweet burn that fits the season. According to the drinksmith, inspiration for the drink's name comes from the treaty that ended the American Revolutionary War and ingredients from three signers of the document: Licor 43 from Spain, Chartreuse from France, and Applejack from America.

> 1/2 ounce Licor 43
> 1/2 ounce Green Chartreuse
> 1 1/2 ounces Laird's Applejack
> 1/2 ounce espresso
> 5 dashes chocolate bitters
> pink Himalayan salt

Combine liquid ingredients in a mixing glass filled with cracked ice. Shake vigorously and strain into a cocktail glass. Sprinkle with salt, to taste.

THE ROYCROFT

A reformist community of craft workers and artists, the Roycrofters formed part of the Arts and Crafts movement in the late nineteenth century. This austere and spirit-forward drink is a tribute to Roycroft craftsmanship, according to Gary Crunkleton of the eponymous Crunkleton Club in Chapel Hill, North Carolina. Its deep amber glow evokes the hue of well-worn wood furniture, and according to the drinksmith, "Their belief of working with your head, hands and heart to create happiness was our inspiration."

> 1 ounce Rittenhouse Bonded Rye Whiskey
> 1 ounce freshly-squeezed lemon juice
> 1/2 ounce Green Chartreuse
> 1/2 ounce Benedictine
> 1/2 ounce Cherry Heering
> 1 thin slice peeled fresh ginger

Combine liquid ingredients in a mixing glass filled with cracked ice. Shake vigorously and strain into a coupe glass. Garnish with ginger.

THE HUNT

"When he folds his hands in slumber before a winter's fire," writes Tom Dolph, "we cry the Hunt and ride with the rushing wind upon the Golden quest." This cocktail, created by Molly Cohen of New York's Rainbow Room, harks back to traditions of the fox, the hound, and the stirrup cup toast. "It's the season for brown spirits and bubbly, and this drink has both," explains the drinksmith. "It's warm and round."

2 ounces bourbon
1 barspoon Green Chartreuse
1 barspoon simple syrup
1 1/2 ounces sparkling apple cider
lemon peel
cinnamon stick

Combine liquid ingredients (except cider) in a mixing glass filled with cracked ice. Stir for 10 seconds and strain into a double Old Fashioned glass over a large ice cube. Top up with cider. Express lemon peel over the glass, rub it around the rim, and drop it in. Garnish with cinnamon stick.

BLACKTHORNE SOUR

Tom Bullock, the son of a former slave and Union soldier, served as bartender at the St. Louis Country Club and in 1917 was the first African-American to publish a cocktail manual. He dedicated *The Ideal Bartender* "To those who enjoy snug club rooms – that they may learn the art of preparing for themselves what is good." Important in the study of cocktail history, his book documents the early use of Chartreuse in mixed drinks..

    1 ounce sloe gin
    1 barspoon pineapple juice
    1/2 barspoon Green Chartreuse
    4 dashes freshly-squeezed lime juice
    lime slice
    pineapple slice

Combine liquid ingredients in a mixing glass filled with cracked ice. Stir for 10 seconds and strain into a cocktail glass. Garnish with fruit slices.

MOOD INDIGO

"Music is the tonal reflection of beauty," said Duke Ellington, whose "Mood Indigo" is a textbook exercise in subtle sophistication. His introspective masterpiece, first recorded in 1930, has been a quintessential jazz/pop standard ever since. Its theme is reflected in the moody composition of apples, spices and herbs, amplified with sparkling wine.

> 1 1/2 ounces Calvados
> 1/4 ounce creme de cassis
> 1/4 ounce Green Chartreuse
> Champagne, chilled
> lemon peel

Combine liquid ingredients (except Champagne) in a mixing glass filled with cracked ice. Stir for 10 seconds and strain into flute glass. Top up with Champagne. Express lemon peel over the glass, rub it around the rim, and discard.

GREEN HORNET

"Kato," says Britt Reid, "we have a secret mission." Reid dons the long green overcoat, green fedora, and green mask of the mysterious Green Hornet on his way to solving another crime. Meanwhile, mixologist Will Herman reveals his own secret recipe for a Chartreuse-spiked, fruit-forward highball.

> 1 ounce Green Chartreuse
> 3/4 ounce freshly-squeezed lime juice
> 4 to 6 ounces pineapple juice
> lime wedge

Fill a highball glass with cracked ice and add Chartreuse. Add lime juice, then fill the glass with pineapple juice. Stir to combine. Garnish with lime wedge.

GREEN EYES

"You're the one that I wanted to find, and anyone who tried to deny you must be out of their mind." The song "Green Eyes," recorded by the Jimmy Dorsey orchestra in 1941 with vocals by Helen O'Connell and Bob Eberly, provides an ideal theme to the two-part harmony of gin and Green Chartreuse by Andrew Volk of Portland Hunt & Alpine in Portland, Maine.

1 1/2 ounces gin
3/4 ounce Green Chartreuse
3/4 ounce freshly-squeezed lime juice
1/2 ounce simple syrup
1/2 ounce egg white
Maraschino cherry
lime slice

Combine ingredients in a mixing glass filled with cracked ice. Dry-shake without ice to combine. Fill with cracked ice and shake vigorously. Double-strain over fresh ice in a rocks glass. Garnish with cherry and lime.

THE METROSEXUAL

According to English journalist Mark Simpson, "Fashions come and go but metrosexuality isn't a fashion – it's an epoch. Although the term has fallen out of use, it's been revived as the name of a drink which resembles a Cosmopolitan, the phenomenally popular vodka cocktail from the dark days of the 1980s. And according to *The Metrosexual Guide to Style*, "nobody stirs Martinis anymore."

> 2 ounces vodka
> 1/4 ounce Green Chartreuse
> 1/8 ounce Cointreau
> orange peel

Combine liquid ingredients in a mixing glass filled with cracked ice. Shake vigorously and strain into a Martini glass. Express orange peel over the glass, rub it around the rim, and drop it in.

RETREAT FROM METROPOLIS

An essential part of the Superman mythos and his home away from home, the icy Arctic fortress provides a place of solace for Superman. The Fortress of Solitude inspires a spirited winter drink with herbal and chocolate notes on a rich base of brandy. It was, of course, Samuel Johnson who famously said: "He who aspires to be a hero must drink brandy."

> 2 ounces brandy
> 3/4 ounce Green Chartreuse
> 1/4 ounce white crème de cacao
> 2 dashes Angostura bitters

Combine ingredients in a mixing glass filled with cracked ice. Stir for 10 seconds and strain into a cocktail glass.

A STUDY IN GREEN

"Art in the blood is liable to take the strangest forms," wrote Sir Arthur Conan Doyle. The creator of Sherlock Holmes, the world's most famous literary detective, was born in Scotland and was a practicing doctor when he began to write tales of mystery and adventure. The artful combination of Scotch and Chartreuse was created in his honor. And as Holmes himself might say, "The game is afoot."

> 1 1/2 ounces Scotch
> 1/2 ounce Green Chartreuse
> 1/4 ounce simple syrup
> 1 dash orange bitters
> star anise

Combine liquid ingredients in a mixing glass filled with cracked ice. Stir for 10 seconds and strain into a cocktail glass. Garnish with star anise.

HAVANA
RAINBOW

Sloppy Joe's Bar in Havana, Cuba, founded by Spanish immigrant José Garcia, capitalized during Prohibition as American tourists and film stars like John Wayne, Spencer Tracy and Clark Gable flocked to the island to drink and gamble to their heart's content. One of Sloppy Joe's specialties, the Rainbow required keeping liquid layers clearly separated to increase the visual appeal.

> 1/4 ounce dark crème de cacao
> 1/4 ounce crème de violette
> 1/4 ounce Yellow Chartreuse
> 1/4 ounce Maraschino liqueur
> 1/4 ounce Benedictine
> 1/4 ounce Green Chartreuse
> 1/4 ounce brandy

In a cordial glass, very slowly pour each individual ingredient over a bar spoon one at a time on top of the last so that they form layers which do not mix with each other. Lightest liquid on top, heaviest on the bottom, etc.

LE DERNIER MOT

The French are incapable of leaving well enough alone. That's what we admire about the mixologists at the Gravity Bar on Rue des Vinaigriers in Paris who tinker with The Last Word. Not only do they use rum in place of gin, but they've decided that lime is the preferred fruit with rum. As in most other variants, Chartreuse and Maraschino remain constant.

> 3/4 ounce rum
> 3/4 ounce Green Chartreuse
> 3/4 ounce Maraschino liqueur
> 3/4 ounce freshly-squeezed lime juice

Combine ingredients in a mixing glass filled with cracked ice. Shake vigorously and double-strain into a cocktail glass.

XANTHIA

The sensual *ménage à trois* of gin, cherry brandy, and Yellow Chartreuse is herbal and fruity, its name derived from the Ancient Greek word Xanthos meaning "yellow," a reference to the yellow hue of the River Xanthos, colored by the soil in the alluvial base of the valley. The cocktail dates back at least to Harry McElhone's 1927 *Barflies and Cocktails*.

> 1 ounce gin
> 1 ounce kirsch
> 1 ounce Yellow Chartreuse

Combine ingredients in a mixing glass filled with cracked ice. Stir for 10 seconds and strain into a cocktail glass.

THE BYWATER

The name refers to one of the oldest neighborhoods of New Orleans. The architectural heritage of Bywater is a rich legacy of Victorian doubles, Creole cottages, Greek Revival and Italian-ate townhouses, and quaint overhanging roofs supported on rows of wooden colonnettes shading the sidewalk. Chris Hannah, one of New Orleans' most beloved bartenders, manning the historic French 75 Bar attached to Arnaud's, turns out a cocktail inspired by the neighborhood's vibe.

> 1 3/4 ounces aged rum
> 3/4 ounce Green Chartreuse
> 1/2 ounce Averna
> 1/4 ounce falernum

Combine ingredients in a mixing glass filled with cracked ice. Stir for 10 seconds and strain into a coupe glass.

BRANDY DAISY

One of the earliest known recipes for the Daisy dates back to 1903 and the publication of *The Flowing Bowl* by Edward Spencer, an Englishman who writes: "The gifts of the gods, and the concoctions of more or less vile man, should be used with moderation." In what is essentially an icy-cold sour with soda water added, the herbal notes of Yellow Chartreuse float lightly above the fullness of the brandy, while the lemon juice cuts the heaviness of the liqueur. Truest to the original.

> juice of 1 lemon
> 1 barspoon powdered sugar
> soda water
> 1 ounce Yellow Chartreuse
> 2 ounces brandy

Combine lemon juice and sugar in the bottom of a mixing glass, and dissolve with a splash of soda water. Add Chatrreuse and brandy. Fill with cracked ice and stir for 10 seconds. Strain into a cocktail glass.

PURGATORY

"If I have to spend time in purgatory before going to one place or the other," said Stephen King, "I guess I'll be all right as long as there's a lending library." In this audacious effort by Ted Kilgore of the Monarch Restaurant in Maplewood, Missouri, Chartreuse and Benedictine are combined in an untortured partnership, finding harmony with the dark nuttiness of the rye whiskey.

> 2 1/2 ounce rye whiskey
> 3/4 ounce Green Chartreuse
> 3/4 ounce Benedictine
> lemon peel

Combine liquid ingredients in a mixing glass filled with cracked ice. Stir for 10 seconds and strain into a coupe glass. Express lemon peel over the glass, rub it around the rim, and drop it in.

GREEN ELEVATOR

Born in Skunk Hollow, New York and educated at Columbia, Crosby Gaige served a brief stint on *The New York Times* before becoming a theatrical agent and producer. Somehow, he found the time to author a couple of books on drinks, including Crosby Gaige's *Cocktail Guide and Ladies' Companion*. In this entry, he tarts up a cocktail that takes herbaceous Chartreuse up to greater heights..

> 1 ounce Green Chartreuse
> juice of 1/2 lemon
> 1/2 ounce grapefruit juice
> 1 egg white

Combine ingredients in a mixing glass filled with cracked ice. Shake vigorously and strain into a coupe glass.

DOUBLE AGENT

"I'm the money," says Vesper Lynd, introducing herself to James Bond. "Every penny of it," he replies. Ian Fleming's cocktail, inspired by his character in 1953's *Casino Royale*, is revamped with the slightly sweet, deeply herbal flavors of Yellow Chartreuse in a drink that can be thought of as yet another improvement of the Martini.

> 2 ounces gin
> 1/4 ounce Yellow Chartrueuse
> 1/4 ounce Lillet Blanc

Combine ingredients in a mixing glass filled with cracked ice. Stir for 10 seconds and strain into a coupe glass.

BOURBON BIJOU

Inspired by the original Bijou dating back to Harry Johnson's 1900 *New and Improved Bartender Manual*, Adam Robinson, mixologist at Park Kitchen in Portland, Oregon swaps gin (a "jewel" in the vintage cocktail) for bourbon, and goes on to prove that Chartreuse can harmonize with whiskey, if you give it a chance. Orange bitters adds a grace note that makes the cocktail sing.

> 2 ounces bourbon
> 1/2 ounce Chartreuse
> 1/2 ounce Punt e Mes
> 2 dashes orange bitters

Combine ingredients in a mixing glass filled with cracked ice. Stir for 10 seconds and strain into a cocktail glass.

DAISY
DE SANTIAGO

The original Cuba Libre and Daiquiri were both created using Bacardi rum, and on his visit to the Bacardi factory, Charles H. Baker Jr. describes this improved Daiquiri as "a lovely thing introduced to us through the gracious offices of the late Facuno Bacardi, of lamented memory." And as for the optional simple syrup, "Personally we find the Chartreuse brings all the sweetening we need," writes Mr. Baker. "A lovely thing indeed."

> 1 1/2 ounces Bacardi rum
> juice of 1 lime
> 1 ounce simple syrup (optional)
> 1/2 ounce Yellow Chartreuse
> mint sprig

Combine liquid ingredients (except Chartreuse) in a mixing glass filled with ice. Stir for 10 seconds and strain into a tall goblet filled with shaved ice. Hold a spoon directly over the drink, rounded side up, and gently pour Yellow Chartreuse over the spoon, creating a "float" on top of the drink. Garnish with mint sprig.

FEAR AND
LOATHING

According to Hunter S. Thompson, "A day without fun is a day that eats shit." The gonzo journalist soaked in a hot tub and sipped Chartreuse to get his creative juices flowing, but once he got started, no topic was safe from his caustic wit. In this tribute to one badass motherfucker, combine Chartreuse, Fernet-Branca and pisco – and let the sparks fly.

> 1 ounce Fernet-Branca
> 3/4 ounce Green Chartreuse
> 1/2 ounce pisco
> lime peel

Combine liquid ingredients in a mixing glass filled with cracked ice. Stir for 10 seconds and strain into a coupe glass. Express lime peel over the glass, rub it around the rim, and drop it in.

MANHATTAN TRANSFER

"Taken sanely and in moderation, whiskey is beneficial, aids digestion, helps throw off colds, megrims, and influenzas," writes Charles Baker in *The Gentleman's Companion*. "Used improperly the effect is just as bad as stuffing on too many starchy foods, taking no exercise, or disliking our neighbor." This aromatic whiskey drink, a variation on the classic Manhattan cocktail is perfumed with floral and violet aromatics.

> 2 ounces rye whiskey
> 1 ounce Punt e Mes vermouth
> 1 barspoon Yellow Chartreuse
> 1 dash Angostura bitters

Combine ingredients in a mixing glass filled with cracked ice. Stir for 10 seconds and strain into a coupe glass.

YELLOW PARROT

"To millions and millions of people all over the world the Stork symbolizes and epitomizes the deluxe upholstery of quintessentially urban existence," pronounced society columnist Lucius Beebe. "It means fame; it means wealth; it means an elegant way of life among celebrated folk." This *ménage à trois* was created in 1935 by barman Albert Coleman at New York's legendary Stork Club.

     1 ounce Yellow Chartreuse
     1 ounce Pernod
     1 ounce apricot brandy

Combine ingredients in a mixing glass filled with cracked ice. Stir for 10 seconds, and strain into a cocktail glass.

TYR'S HAND

It's baptized after the one-handed god of war in Viking Age mythology. Repurposing the Rusty Nail, Shawn Beck of Berlin's Redwood Bar replaces the heavy sweetness of Drambuie with Yellow Chartreuse, and adding sherry provides nutty complexity. Is the big cube necessary? "No," says Mr. Beck, "but it's more aesthetically pleasing."

2 ounces of Buffalo Trace bourbon
1 ounce Amontillado sherry
1/2 ounce of Yellow Chartreuse
1 dash orange bitters
orange peel

Combine liquid ingredients in an Old Fashioned glass and add a large ice cube. Stir. Express the orange peel over the drink and place on top of the ice cube.

AIDE MEMOIR

"Memory," wrote Oscar Wilde, "is the diary that we all carry about with us." Its name a play on *aide-mémoire,* French for a memory aid, a document that helps you remember something important, this formula from Jason Walsh of Bea in New York City is a balance of sweet and bitter with a float of Prosecco for a celebratory air.

> 1 1/2 ounces Carpano Antica
> 1/2 ounce Yellow Chartreuse
> 1 dash orange bitters
> Prosecco, chilled
> orange peel

Combine liquid ingredients in a mixing glass filled with cracked ice. Shake vigorously and strain into a coupe glass. Top with Prosecco. Express orange peel over the glass, rub it around the rim, and drop it in.

GYPSY WOMAN

Scented with the aroma of jasmine blossoms, gin melds with fresh lime juice, St. Germain elderflower liqueur and Yellow Chartreuse in this enchantingly floral cocktail from a menu of French-influenced tipples created by barkeep Justin Noel at 1534, the subterranean space beneath Jacques in New York City. Quite pleasant indeed.

> 2 ounces tea-infused gin*
> 3/4 ounce freshly-squeezed lime juice
> 1/2 ounce St. Germain elderflower liqueur
> 1/2 ounce Yellow Chartreuse
> lemon peel

Combine liquid ingredients in a mixing glass filled with cracked ice. Shake vigorously and double strain into coupe glass. Express lemon peel over the glass, rub it around the rim, and drop it in.

*Pour 10 ounces gin into re-sealable jar and add 2 green tea bags. Infuse at room temperature for 1 hour, taste for flavor, then continue to infuse up to 2 hours more if desired, tasting every 30 minutes. Remove tea bags and reseal.

THE SCOFFLAW

In 1923, Delcevare King, a supporter of Prohibition announced a $200 prize to anyone who created a term that best expressed "the idea of lawless drinker, menace, bad citizen." Over 25,000 entries later, "scofflaw" was the winner, and the following year a bartender known only as "Jock," debuted his cocktail recipe at Harry's Bar in Paris. Poking fun at the folly of the American Prohibition, he called it the Scofflaw Cocktail. The formula first appeared in Patrick Gavin Duffy's 1934 *Official Mixer's Manual*. (Originally the Scofflaw was made with grenadine, but a later version called for Chartreuse instead – more herbal, less sweet).

> 1 ounce rye whiskey
> 1 ounce French vermouth
> 3/4 ounce Green Chartreuse
> 3/4 ounce freshly-squeezed lemon juice
> 1 dash orange bitters
> lemon peel, for garnish

Combine liquid ingredients in a mixing glass filled with cracked ice. Shake vigorously and strain into a cocktail glass. Express lemon peel over the glass, rub it around the rim, and drop it in.

PEPPERBOX

The Prohibition-era Last Word cocktail, developed at the Detroit Athletic Club during the 1920s, provides inspiration for a gin-forward revision at the Red Feather Lounge in Boise, Idaho. The taste varies slightly depending on the brand of gin being used; Plymouth provides fresh juniper and lemony bite. The palate is at once a little sour, a little sweet, and a little pungent.

> 2 ounces Plymouth gin
> 1/2 ounce Green Chartreuse
> 1/2 ounce freshly-squeezed lime juice
> 1 dash simple syrup
> peppered lemon peel

Combine ingredients in a mixing glass filled with cracked ice. Shake vigorously and strain into a coupe glass. Grind fresh pepper onto lemon peel and drop on the surface of the drink.

WIDOW'S KISS

First published in George Kappeler's *Modern American Drinks* in 1895, this well-matched set of ingredients disappeared into the vacuum of Prohibition. Ted Haigh, the inimitable Dr. Cocktail, compares the taste of the Widow's Kiss to the feeling of finding in a dusty attic old love letters wrapped in lace in your grand-mother's 1914 suitcase.

> 1 1/2 ounces Calvados
> 3/4 ounce Yellow Chartreuse
> 3/4 ounce Benedictine
> 2 dashes Angostura bitters
> brandied cherry

Combine liquid ingredients in a mixing glass filled with cracked ice. Stir for 10 seconds, and strain into a cocktail glass. Drop cherry into the bottom of the glass.

THE MAY QUEEN

The master chronicler of upper-class British buffoonery, P. G. Wodehouse's best-known contribution to the culture of drinking is his recipe from *Uncle Fred in the Springtime*. According to cocktail historian Scott C. Martin, the drink provides a sort of enhanced "Dutch courage" to its imbibers, inspiring them to propose marriage.

> 3/4 ounce brandy
> 3/4 ounce Armagnac
> 3/4 ounce Kümmel
> 3/4 ounce Yellow Chartreuse
> Champagne, chilled
> stout, to taste

Add brandy, Armagnac, Kümmel, and Yellow Chartreuse to a Champagne glass. Fill to 1/2-inch of the rim with Champagne. Top up with stout.

REBEL WITH A CAUSE

According to Ted Haigh (aka Dr. Cocktail), drinking Fernet-Branca is "something of a rebellious statement, because it has a striking bitterness. It became notorious in biker bars where bikers would down it to show how tough they were, much as Hemingway drank Ng Ka Py." Chartreuse becomes a partner-in-crime, lending complexity to this strong, spirits-forward sipper.

> 1 ounce Fernet-Branca
> 3/4 ounce Green Chartreuse
> 1/2 ounce pisco
> lime peel

Combine liquid ingredients in a mixing glass filled with cracked ice. Stir for 10 seconds, and strain into a cocktail glass. Express lime peel over the glass, rub it around the rim, and discard.

CRIMES AND MISDEMEANORS

Proportion is that agreeable harmony between the elements of a cocktail, in which no single flavor dominates the others. Rye and vermouth become equal partners to the Chartreuse and Fernet-Branca, and on the palate, seemingly combative ingredients together reach unexpected accord. A mighty strong, alcohol-forward drink.

    1 ounce rye whiskey
    1/2 ounce French vermouth
    1 ounce Green Chartreuse
    1/2 ounce Fernet-Branca
    1 dash Angostura bitters
    lemon peel

Combine liquid ingredients in a mixing glass filled with cracked ice. Stir for 10 seconds and strain over fresh ice cubes in a double old-fashioned glass. Express lemon peel over the glass, rub it around the rim, and drop it in.

ORTO BOTANICO

A magical place, where massive statues guide visitors along a path to reach a secret garden, Milan's "Orto Botanico," originally used in the 17th century by the Jesuits to grow and teach others about medicinal plants, provides inspiration for a botanically-rich, almost hypnotic variation of the classic Negroni. After all, a garden always has a point.

> 1 1/4 ounces Campari
> 1 ounce gin
> 1/2 ounce Green Chartreuse
> 1/2 ounce French vermouth
> 1/4 ounce Fernet-Branca
> lemon peel

Combine liquid ingredients in a mixing glass filled with cracked ice. Shake vigorously and strain into a cocktail glass. Express lemon peel over the glass, rub it around the rim, and drop it in.

LA DAME VERTE

One of the most infamous residents of the Loire Valley's Château de Brissac, La Dame Verte (the Green Lady) is said to be the ghost of a woman by the name of Charlotte de Brézé, the illegitimate daughter of King Charles VII and his mistress, Agnes Sorel. This variation on the classics Pink Lady and White Lady calls for Green Chartreuse instead of grenadine or Cointreau.

> 1 1/2 ounces gin
> 3/4 ounce Green Chartreuse
> 1/2 ounce freshly-squeezed lime juice
> 1 egg white

Combine ingredients in a mixing glass. Dry shake. Fill with cracked ice, shake vigorously, and strain into a cocktail glass.

THE LUMIÈRE

This magical sophistication of elderflower, citrus, and Chartreuse is the creation of Jen Marshall of Nitehawk Cinema in New York City, inspired by Martin Scorsese's 2011 film *Hugo*, an homage to French filmmakers Auguste and Louis Lumière, and a love letter to Paris in the 1930s.

1 1/2 ounces gin
1 ounce St. Germain elderflower liqueur
3/4 ounce freshly-squeezed lime juice
3/4 ounce Green Chartreuse
1 dash bitters
lime peel

Combine liquid ingredients in a mixing glass filled with cracked ice. Stir for 10 seconds and strain into a coupe glass. Express lime peel over the glass, rub it around the rim, and discard.

WARDAY'S COCKTAIL

As transatlantic travel became more popular in the late 19th and early 20th centuries, many American-style bars opened throughout London. Warday himself was likely one of barman Harry Craddock's favored customers at the Savoy Hotel's American Bar, and his preferred sipper was this herbaceous, yet elegant blend of gin, Calvados, sweet vermouth, and Yellow Chartreuse – immortalized in Craddock's *Savoy Cocktail Book*.

1 ounce gin
1 ounce Calvados
1 ounce Italian vermouth
1 barspoon Green Chartreuse
lemon peel

Combine ingredients in a mixing glass filled with cracked ice. Stir for 10 seconds and strain into a coupe glass. Express lime peel over the glass, rub it around the rim, and drop it in.

THE GRAPES OF WRATH

"There ain't no sin and there ain't no virtue," wrote John Steinbeck in *The Grapes of Wrath.* "There's just stuff people do." Matthew Biancaniello of New York's Roosevelt Hotel Bar ingeniously muddles Concord grapes with simple syrup and fresh lemon to release their sweet, tangy, fragrant pulp. The distinctive fruit flavor harmonizes the partnership of gin and Chartreuse.

> 4 fresh Concord grapes
> 3/4 ounce freshly-squeezed lemon juice
> 1/2 ounce simple syrup
> 1 1/2 ounces gin
> 1/2 ounce Green Chartreuse

One by one, hold each grape between thumb and forefinger. Squeeze gently so the grape slips out of its skin. Discard the skin and set aside the grape. Repeat with the remaining grapes. Cut the grapes in half and dig out the seed from each grape. Muddle the grapes with the lemon juice and simple syrup in the bottom of a rocks glass. Add the gin, Chartreuse and 3 ice cubes. Stir and serve with a julep spoon straw.

THE
ALAMAGOOZLUM

J. Pierpont Morgan, the financier and banker, took his daily af-ter-work drink at the Waldorf-Astoria hotel, as did all the thirsty young men who aspired to his throne. Legend holds that it was Morgan himself who invented the Alamagoozlum, a cocktail whose formula allowed the individual drinker to choose his or her preferred version of Chartreuse among ingredients – Yellow Chartreuse option providing the path to a milder cocktail.

> 1/2 egg white
> 1 ounce Genever
> 3/4 ounce Jamaican rum
> 3/4 ounce Chartreuse (Green or Yellow)
> 3/4 ounce simple syrup
> 1/4 ounce orange Curacao
> 3 dashes Angostura bitters
> soda water

Add ingredients (except soda water) to a mixing glass filled with cracked ice. Shake vigorously and strain over new ice in a tall glass. Finish with a splash of soda water.

VERTE CHAUD

In the French Alps *après-ski*, a mug of Verte Chaude often awaits. At the Monkey Bar in the village of Chamonix, a resort on north side of the summit of Mont Blanc, the most popular libation is a Chartreuse-spiked rich hot chocolate, guaranteed to warm the body inside and out, finished with a "white mountain" of whipped cream. The essence of the drink is diving through the cold cream to the warm underbelly.

> 4 1/2 ounces hot chocolate*
> 1 1/2 ounces Green Chartreuse
> heavy cream, whipped to soft peaks

Combine hot chocolate and Chartreuse in a warmed cup. Top with whipped cream.

*In a small saucepan set over medium-high heat, bring 6 ounces of whole milk, 2 ounces of heavy cream, and 1 teaspoon confectioners' sugar to a simmer together, heating just until bubbles appear around the edges of the liquid. Remove the pan from the heat and add chocolate, stirring to melt it completely. If necessary, return the pan to low heat while stirring constantly with a wooden spoon until the chocolate is melted. The mixture should appear smooth and evenly colored.

GREEN DRAGON

According to *The Esquire Drink Book*, a "complete guide to high spirits," the green of Chartreuse is "the color decorators have copped onto." The 1956 cocktail guide includes this recipe for layering "good French brandy" over Chartreuse to enhance the tone of the sip. (In the alternative, a float of Cognac over Yellow Chartreuse is called a Golden Dragon).

> 1/4 ounce Cognac
> 3/4 ounce Green Chartreuse

Add Chartreuse to a brandy cordial glass. Hold a spoon directly over the drink, rounded side up, and gently pour Cognac over the spoon, creating a "float" on top of the drink.

THE QUEEN'S ENGLISH

Queen Elizabeth of England is very much a creature of habit. Every evening, it has been reported, she drinks a glass or two of Champagne spiked with Chartreuse. The only question is why this herbal cocktail hasn't got a Royal Warrant. Maybe because it's French.

> 3/4 ounce Green Chartreuse
> Champagne, chilled
> 1 dash Maraschino liqueur

Add Chartreuse to a Champagne flute. Fill to 1/2-inch of the rim with Champagne. Top with a dash of Maraschino liqueur.

EPISCOPALE

Green or yellow, Chartreuse is forever engulfed in mystery. Despite their differences, the sister spirits can be paired together in an after-dinner sipper that has the warming, herbaceous, complex characters for which the monks first brewed the spirit, but with a softer, sweeter taste profile and milder aromatics.

1 1/2 ounces Yellow Chartreuse
3/4 ounce Green Chartreuse

Combine ingredients in a mixing glass filled with cracked ice. Stir for 10 seconds and strain over new ice in a rocks glass.

ESPRIT

Chartreuse evolves depending on its temperature, and many bartenders suggest keeping the bottle in the freezer where it becomes thick and viscous, the chill calming a bit of the fire. Pour a shot of Green Chartreuse neat, hold the glass up to your nose, take a deep breath, and savor the aroma. "One sip of this will bathe the drooping spirits in delight, beyond the bliss of dreams," writes John Milton. And in the words of Caroline Knapp, "To a drinker the sensation is real and pure and akin to something spiritual."

2 ounces Green Chartreuse, chilled

Add Chartreuse to a brandy snifter. Consume with reverence.

A FEW PAGES
FOR YOUR
OWN RECIPES

Made in the USA
Columbia, SC
26 June 2019